Why Do Rabbits Hop?

And Other Questions about Rabbits, Guinea Pigs, Hamsters, and Gerbils

by JOAN HOLUB

illustrations by Anna DiVito

Dial Books for Young Readers • New York

Published by Dial Books for Young Readers
A division of Penguin Putnam Inc.
345 Hudson Street
New York, New York 10014

Printed in Hong Kong

The Dial Easy-to-Read logo is a registered trademark of Dial Books for Young Readers,
a division of Penguin Putnam Inc.
® TM 1,162,718.

1 3 5 7 9 10 8 6 4 2

LIBRARY OF CONGRESS CATALOGING-IN-PUBLICATION DATA

Holub, Joan.
Why do rabbits hop? : and other questions about rabbits, guinea
pigs, hamsters, and gerbils / by Joan Holub ; illustrations by Anna DiVito.
p. cm.
Summary: Questions and answers present information about the
behavior and characteristics of rabbits, guinea pigs, hamsters, and
gerbils and their interaction with humans.
ISBN 0-8037-2771-2–ISBN 0-14-230120-5 (pbk.)
1. Rabbits–Miscellanea—Juvenile literature. 2. Guinea pigs as pets—
Miscellanea—Juvenile literature. 3. Hamsters as pets–Miscellanea—Juvenile literature.
4. Gerbils as pets–Miscellanea—Juvenile literature. [1. Rabbits as pets—Miscellanea.
2. Guinea pigs as pets—Miscellanea. 3. Hamsters as pets—Miscellanea.
4. Gerbils as pets–Miscellanea. 5. Questions and answers.]
I. DiVito, Anna, ill. II. Title.
SF416.2 .H66 2003
636.9'322—dc21 2001047477

Reading Level 2.5

Photo Credits

Note: The information in this book is not complete and is not intended to provide professional
advice regarding appropriate care, food, housing, toys, or games for your pet, or advice concerning
the suitability of any of these pets for your family. Consult your pet store and vet for more complete
information about the pets in this book before purchasing these pets or any supplies for them.
These pets may bite, scratch, or provoke allergic reactions. Consult your doctor in the event of
injury or allergic reaction. It is inadvisable to try and tame wild animals to become pets. Review
state, city, and local laws in your area before purchasing one of these pets, since it is illegal to own
some of the animals mentioned in this book in some locations.

*For Kristin Gilson and Tracy Tang with
many thanks*—J.H.

For Emma and Chris—A.D.

Many people like rabbits,

guinea pigs, hamsters, and gerbils.

They are small, soft, cute,

and playful.

They do not need a lot of space

or cost a lot of money.

They are easier to care for than

larger pets such as cats or dogs.

rabbit

hamster

guinea pig

gerbil

Are all of these animals rodents?

Guinea pigs, hamsters, and gerbils
are members of the rodent family.
Rodents are small mammals.
Some other rodents are mice, rats,
squirrels, and chipmunks.
All rodents have four sharp front teeth,
two on top and two on bottom,
as well as smaller back teeth.

Your front teeth stop growing

when they are the right size.

A rodent's front teeth

never stop growing.

Their teeth can grow

up to several inches a year!

Rabbits are not rodents.

They have six sharp front teeth,

instead of just four.

But like rodents, their front teeth

never stop growing.

Why don't rabbits' and rodents' teeth grow down to the ground?

These animals chew on objects like sticks

or blocks to wear their teeth down.

It would be hard for them to eat

if their teeth grew too long.

Since rabbits and rodents will try to chew

on almost anything, it is important to be

sure that they are kept away from things

that might harm them.

What do rabbits, guinea pigs, hamsters, and gerbils eat?

In the wild, these animals

eat fruits, vegetables, and hay.

You can feed your pet snacks

such as carrots and apples,

as well as dry food from a pet store.

There are different kinds of dry food

for each animal.

Some foods can make them sick,

so ask your vet or pet store

which foods are best for your pet.

Rabbits

How many different kinds of rabbits are there?

There are about fifty breeds,

or kinds, of rabbits.

Rabbits can be big or small.

They come in different colors.

Their fur can be long or short.

The Himalayan (him-ah-LAY-an)

is a popular pet rabbit

because it is small and easygoing.

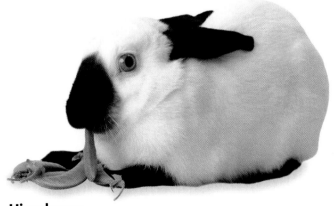

Himalayan

What are the smallest and biggest rabbits?

The smallest breed of rabbit is the

Netherland Dwarf.

They weigh only two pounds.

The biggest rabbits are Flemish Giants.

They can weigh over twenty-two pounds!

That is about the same weight

as a one-year-old human.

Netherland Dwarf

Flemish Giant

How many babies can a rabbit have?

A mother rabbit usually has four to
eight babies at a time.
She can have babies as often as
three times a year.
A baby rabbit is sometimes called a
kitten, but most people call them bunnies.

What are baby rabbits like?

A newborn baby rabbit

weighs only about two ounces.

That is the same weight as ten quarters.

A baby rabbit is born without fur.

Its fur begins to grow when it is

four days old.

It is also born with its eyes closed.

They open after ten days.

A baby rabbit drinks milk from its mother.

When it is about three weeks old,

it also begins to eat other foods.

A rabbit can leave its mother

when it is eight weeks old.

Which rabbit has the longest ears?

A breed of rabbit called the Lop

has the longest ears.

The ears of some Lops can grow

up to twenty-six inches long!

The word "lop" means to hang down.

Lop rabbits' ears hang down

instead of pointing up.

Do rabbits like to be picked up by their ears?

Never pick a rabbit up by its ears.

That will hurt the tiny bones

and muscles in its ears.

Hold a rabbit gently and firmly,

so it will feel safe.

This picture shows a good way to

hold a rabbit.

Why do rabbits hop?

Rabbits can't walk or run
like many other animals can.
A rabbit's strong legs and big back feet
are made for hopping.
Rabbits can hop as fast as twenty
miles an hour.
They can jump up to ten feet in one hop!
In the wild, rabbits will hop in a
zigzag pattern to get away from animals
that are chasing them.

Can rabbits climb?

Rabbits can't climb very high.
So they aren't able to climb trees
to escape danger.
But rabbits can stand very still.
When they do this, they are trying to
camouflage (CAM-o-flahj) themselves.
This means they are trying to blend in
with what's around them so that
they won't be seen by other animals.

How do rabbits communicate?

Rabbits do not make a lot of noise.

They may lightly grind their teeth

or hum softly if they are happy.

When angry, they may bite or growl.

Rabbits' actions also show how they feel.

Sometimes a rabbit will rub its chin
on a cage, toy, or person.
This leaves a special smell behind.
People can't smell it,
but other rabbits can.
This special smell tells other rabbits,
"This is mine."
Rabbits stomp their back feet
when they are scared.
They kick their legs or jump up
to show they are happy.

Do rabbits like to play?

Rabbits are curious, and they like

to play with simple toys.

Empty paper-towel rolls and

small cardboard boxes

make good toys for a rabbit.

Rabbits also like to dig in hay

or shredded paper.

They like to chew and scratch

objects made of cardboard or wood.

Rabbits sleep most of the day,

so they may only want to play

in the morning or evening.

Do rabbits like company?

A rabbit can get lonely

when it lives in a cage by itself.

But two rabbits living

in one cage may fight.

Two girl rabbits will get along

better than two boys.

A rabbit and a guinea pig

can make good roommates!

Are rabbits smart?

Rabbits are smart and trainable.

Rabbits can learn to recognize

their names and other words.

Some rabbits can learn to open

cage doors.

Rabbits can even be taught

to use a litter box!

Guinea Pigs

Is a guinea pig a pig?

People are not sure how guinea
pigs got their name.
The first guinea pigs came
from South America.
The word "guinea" may refer to Guiana,
a country in South America.
Or it may refer to the fact
that guinea pigs were once sold
for one guinea (an old English coin).
Guinea pigs are rodents, not pigs.
They might have been called pigs
because they grunt and squeal like pigs.
Another name for a guinea pig
is a cavy (KAY-vee).

How many babies can a guinea pig have?

A mother guinea pig has one to four babies at a time.

She can have babies as often as four times a year.

A baby guinea pig is called a pup.

What are baby guinea pigs like?

When guinea pigs are born, their eyes are already open, and they are covered with fur.

They can walk and play

on the same day they are born!

Guinea pigs drink milk

from their mother for a few weeks.

But they also eat other foods

within a few days of birth.

They can leave their mother

when they are about six weeks old.

Adult guinea pigs are eight to

twelve inches long,

and weigh two or three pounds.

They are about the same size and

shape as an adult's sneaker!

How do guinea pigs communicate?

Guinea pigs are gentle and friendly,

but they are noisy!

They grunt, squeak, or whistle

when they want food or attention.

They also grunt when they are happy.

Guinea pigs sometimes purr and coo

to their babies, to each other,

or to people they like.

A guinea pig will squeal when it is scared or hurt.

If it chatters its teeth, watch out!

It is angry.

Guinea pigs' actions also show how they feel.

To say hello, guinea pigs bump noses.

When it is afraid, a guinea pig may lie very still on its back.

It is pretending to be dead so that another animal won't attack it.

Do guinea pigs like to play?

Guinea pigs like to play hide-and-seek. They hide beneath the wood shavings and hay inside their cages.

Guinea pigs enjoy simple toys such as a cardboard toilet-paper roll, a paper cup, or a small plain cardboard box.

Like you, guinea pigs like to play during the day and sleep at night. But they take short daytime naps, too.

Do guinea pigs get along?

Guinea pigs can get lonely.

They like to live with other guinea pigs.

Two girl guinea pigs usually get along

better than two boys do.

Can guinea pigs see, smell, and hear well?

Guinea pigs can see well,

but they know other guinea pigs

and people best by the way they smell.

Guinea pigs also have good hearing.

They can hear high-pitched sounds

that people can't hear.

If you have a guinea pig,
it may learn the sound of
your footsteps.
It will get excited when it hears
you coming.

Hamsters

Gerbils

How are hamsters and gerbils different?

Many people confuse hamsters and gerbils, but there are differences.

A hamster is six to seven inches long and has a very short, stubby tail.

A gerbil is about four inches long.

Its tail is as long as its body.

Gerbils are better jumpers than hamsters.

Both animals can hear and smell well, but gerbils have better eyesight.

Hamsters like to live alone.

Gerbils like to live with other gerbils.

Hamsters have pouches in their cheeks, and gerbils don't.

Where do hamsters and gerbils come from?

Golden hamsters are

the most popular kind of pet hamster.

The first golden hamsters were

found in a part of Asia

called Syria (SEAR-ee-ah) around 1930.

The most popular kind of pet gerbil

is the Mongolian (mon-GOH-lee-an) gerbil.

The first Mongolian gerbils came

from the Mongolian Desert in Asia.

Golden hamster

When do hamsters and gerbils sleep?

Mongolian gerbils sleep at night.

They are awake most of the day,

but do take short naps every few hours.

Golden hamsters sleep during the day

and are awake at night.

They sleep fourteen hours a day.

How many hours do you sleep?

Mongolian gerbil

How many babies can a hamster or gerbil have?

Mother hamsters have

about seven babies at a time.

Mother gerbils have

about five babies at a time.

Baby hamsters and gerbils

are called pups.

What are baby hamsters and gerbils like?

Newborn hamsters and gerbils are pink.

They weigh one-tenth of an ounce.

That is about the same weight as a pencil!

Newborn hamsters and gerbils

don't have fur, and they can't see.

Their fur begins to grow within a few days.

Their eyes open in about two weeks.

They drink milk from their mothers

until they are about three weeks old.

How do hamsters and gerbils communicate?

Hamsters and gerbils are quiet animals.

But they can make sounds

and do things to show how they feel.

They may squeak softly

to talk to other hamsters or gerbils.

Hamsters may hiss, squeal, or growl

when they are angry or scared.

Hamsters and gerbils may leap in the air

if they are happy or surprised.

Gerbils thump the ground

with their hind legs

to show they are excited

or to tell other animals to stay away.

Why do hamsters have cheek pouches?

Hamsters have special pouches

in their cheeks that allow them to carry

things without swallowing them.

To save food for later,

hamsters stuff it into their cheek pouches.

When they find a hiding place,

they use their front paws

to push the food out of the pouches.

Then they bury the food in the
hiding place, and dig it up when
they are ready to eat it.

When a hamster's cheek pouches are full,
its head can look twice as big as usual!
Sometimes hamsters even carry their
newborn babies in their cheek pouches.
This doesn't hurt the babies at all.

What toys do hamsters and gerbils like?

They like exercise wheels, ladders,

steps, swings, seesaws, tunnels,

and wooden toys.

They will get bored with the same toy

after a while.

Hamster and gerbil tricks:

1. Put a sunflower seed in your shirt pocket, and let your hamster or gerbil search for it.
After a few times, your pet will learn to climb up your arm and look in your pocket for a treat.

2. Build a maze with blocks. Put a treat in the center.
Set your pet at the entrance and watch it find its way to the food.
Does it find its way more easily the second time?

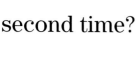

Pet rabbits, guinea pigs,
hamsters, and gerbils need
food, water, and exercise every day.
It may take a few weeks before your
pet trusts you enough to eat from
your hand or to let you pick it up.
Speak softly and be gentle.
Be a good friend to these pets,
and they will be good friends to you.